Typing Lesson Beginners

MW00413080

Quick way to learn English Typing

Shiva G

Copyright ©2007 – 2017 by

GSPublication

ISBN Number : ISBN: 9781973447726

Publication Address
CGS Infotech,

GS Publication,

3/4, Anna salai, Near Vasavai Mahal,

Rasipuram Tk, Namakkal Dist,

Tamilnadu – 637408

Why I wrote this Book

- This book useful to who wants to learn keyboard typing without seeing the keyboard
- Today computer and internet used by each and every one. but most of them struggle to type characters. They search every characters while typing. It will take more time to finish single page of document. So i plan to teach the typing method in proper manner
- If you are follow the lesson and practice in your home or office 30 minutes per day I assure you. definetly you will become a master of keyboard typing. This is my aim who purchase this book they will become a good in typing master in keyboard
- If you practiced all the lessons, once again start from lesson1 to end of the lesson You will see your keyboard fingering mistakes are reduced
- Practice makes a man perfect.So continuously practice it, to become a master of keys.
- I assure you. If you complete the lessons properly then you love the keys while typing

Table of contents

Keyboard Characters

Key Structure Model

Original Keyboard

Lesson – 1 (Base Row)

How to use (Base Row)

A S D F and **; L K J** are called to be a guidelines characters.

Keep on your mind:
- Always keep your fingers on **A S D F** and **; L K J**
- While Typing Base Row characters don't see keyboard.
- Your Eyes only focus on moniter
- If you done any mistakes don't try to correct. Just leave your mistakes and continue your fingering on keyboard
- Care about that mistakenly typed characters to reduce your mistakes

Left Hand Finger Positions
Keep your Left hand finger on keyboard at the position of ...

Little finger on.........   : **A**

Ring finger on ....   : **S**

Middle finger on ...   : **D**

Index finger on .....   : **F**

Right Hand Finger Positions
Keep your Right hand finger on keyboard at the position of ...

Little finger on.........   : **;**

Ring finger on ....   : **L**

Middle finger on ...   : **K**

Index finger on ..... : J

Thumb finger on .....: Space Bar

Left Hand Finger Position Image

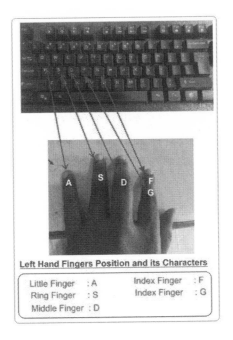

Left Hand Fingers Position and its Characters

Little Finger	: A	Index Finger	: F
Ring Finger	: S	Index Finger	: G
Middle Finger	: D		

Right Hand Finger Position Image

Right Hand Fingers Position and its Characters

Little Finger	: ;	Index Finger	: J
Ring Finger	: L	Index Finger	: H
Middle Finger	: K		

Exercise 1 (asdf ;lkj)

Repeat the following 25 lines:

asdf ;lkj asdf ;lkj asdf ;lkj asdf ;lkj asdf ;lkj asdf ;lkj asdf ;lkj
asdf ;lkj asdf ;lkj asdf ;lkj asdf ;lkj asdf ;lkj asdf ;lkj asdf ;lkj
asdf ;lkj asdf ;lkj asdf ;lkj asdf ;lkj asdf ;lkj asdf ;lkj asdf ;lkj
asdf ;lkj asdf ;lkj asdf ;lkj asdf ;lkj asdf ;lkj asdf ;lkj asdf ;lkj

asdf ;lkj asdf ;lkj asdf ;lkj asdf ;lkj asdf ;lkj asdf ;lkj asdf ;lkj
asdf ;lkj asdf ;lkj asdf ;lkj asdf ;lkj asdf ;lkj asdf ;lkj asdf ;lkj
asdf ;lkj asdf ;lkj asdf ;lkj asdf ;lkj asdf ;lkj asdf ;lkj asdf ;lkj
asdf ;lkj asdf ;lkj asdf ;lkj asdf ;lkj asdf ;lkj asdf ;lkj asdf ;lkj

Exercise 2 (asdfgf ;lkjhj)

asdfgf ;lkjhj asdfgf ;lkjhj asdfgf ;lkjhj asdfgf ;lkjhj asdfgf ;lkjhj
asdfgf ;lkjhj asdfgf ;lkjhj asdfgf ;lkjhj asdfgf ;lkjhj asdfgf ;lkjhj
asdfgf ;lkjhj asdfgf ;lkjhj asdfgf ;lkjhj asdfgf ;lkjhj asdfgf ;lkjhj
asdfgf ;lkjhj asdfgf ;lkjhj asdfgf ;lkjhj asdfgf ;lkjhj asdfgf ;lkjhj

asdfgf ;lkjhj asdfgf ;lkjhj asdfgf ;lkjhj asdfgf ;lkjhj asdfgf ;lkjhj
asdfgf ;lkjhj asdfgf ;lkjhj asdfgf ;lkjhj asdfgf ;lkjhj asdfgf ;lkjhj
asdfgf ;lkjhj asdfgf ;lkjhj asdfgf ;lkjhj asdfgf ;lkjhj asdfgf ;lkjhj
asdfgf ;lkjhj asdfgf ;lkjhj asdfgf ;lkjhj asdfgf ;lkjhj asdfgf ;lkjhj

asdfgf ;lkjhj asdfgf ;lkjhj asdfgf ;lkjhj asdfgf ;lkjhj asdfgf ;lkjhj
asdfgf ;lkjhj asdfgf ;lkjhj asdfgf ;lkjhj asdfgf ;lkjhj asdfgf ;lkjhj
asdfgf ;lkjhj asdfgf ;lkjhj asdfgf ;lkjhj asdfgf ;lkjhj asdfgf ;lkjhj
asdfgf ;lkjhj asdfgf ;lkjhj asdfgf ;lkjhj asdfgf ;lkjhj asdfgf ;lkjhj

Exercise 3 (Base Row Exercises)

Practicing Method Example

ask ask ask ask ask ask ask ask ask ask ask ask ask ask
ask ask ask ask ask ask ask ask ask ask ask ask ask ask
ask ask ask ask ask ask ask ask ask ask ask ask ask ask
ask ask ask ask ask ask ask ask ask ask ask ask ask ask

all all all all all all all all all all all all all all all all all all
all all all all all all all all all all all all all all all all all all
all all all all all all all all all all all all all all all all all all
all all all all all all all all all all all all all all all all all all

ash ash ash ash ash ash ash ash ash ash ash ash ash
ash ash ash ash ash ash ash ash ash ash ash ash ash
ash ash ash ash ash ash ash ash ash ash ash ash ash
ash ash ash ash ash ash ash ash ash ash ash ash ash

aga aga aga aga aga aga aga aga aga aga aga aga aga aga
aga aga aga aga aga aga aga aga aga aga aga aga aga aga
aga aga aga aga aga aga aga aga aga aga aga aga aga aga
aga aga aga aga aga aga aga aga aga aga aga aga aga aga

Repeat each word 4 lines

(Follow the example given above)

1) ask	2) all	3) ash	4) aga
5) add	6) sag	7) sal	8) sad
9) sad	10) dad	11) dak	12) fag
13) fad	14) gas	15) gad	16) gag
17) had	18) has	19) hag	20) hah
21) jag	22) lads	23) lags	24) lass
25) alas	26) adds	27) shad	28) shah
29) daff	30) dhall	31) flash	32) lakhs

Lesson – 2 (Upper Row)

How to use (Upper Row)

Q W E R T and **P O I U Y** are called to be a upper row Keys.

Keep on your mind:

- Always keep your fingers on **A S D F** and **; L K J.**
- While you are pressing upper row key, use only corresponding finger. Don't move all the fingers to top row.
- Your fingers always kept on **A S D F** and **; L K J** positions.
- While Typing Top Row characters don't see keyboard.
- Your Eyes only focus on moniter
- If you done any mistakes don't try to correct. Just leave your mistakes and continue your fingering on keyboard
- Care about that mistakenly typed characters to reduce your mistakes

Typing Method

Left Hand Fingers

a – Left little finger   w – Left ring finger

e – Left middle finger   r – Left index finger

q – Left little finger   f – Left index finger

a – Left little finger

Right Hand fingers

; - Right little finger   o - Right ring finger

i - Right middle finger u - Right index finger

p - Right little finger   j - Right index finger   ; - Right little finger

Left Hand Finger Keys Image

Left Hand Fingers Position and its Characters

Little Finger	: A	Index Finger	: R
Ring Finger	: W	Index Finger	: T
Middle Finger	: E		

Right Hand Finger Keys Image

Right Hand Fingers Position and its Characters

Little Finger	: P	Index Finger	: U
Ring Finger	: O	Index Finger	: Y
Middle Finger	: I		

Left Hand Finger Keys on top row

Keep your Left hand finger on keyboard at the position of ... A and Right hand finger on keyboard ;

Little finger on........   : **Q**

Ring finger on ....   : **W**

Middle finger on ...   : **E**

Index finger on .....   : **R**

Right Hand Finger Keys on top row

Keep your Right hand finger on keyboard at the position of ... A and Right hand finger on keyboard ;

Little Finger Key ...   : **P**

Ring finger Key ……. : **O**

Middle finger Key … : **I**

Index finger Key ….. : **U**

Exercise 4 (awerqfa, ;oiupj;)

Repeat the following 25 lines:

awerqfa ;oiupj; awerqfa ;oiupj; awerqfa ;oiupj; awerqfa
awerqfa ;oiupj; awerqfa ;oiupj; awerqfa ;oiupj; awerqfa
awerqfa ;oiupj; awerqfa ;oiupj; awerqfa ;oiupj; awerqfa
awerqfa ;oiupj; awerqfa ;oiupj; awerqfa ;oiupj; awerqfa

Exercise 5 (Top Row Exercises)

Practicing Method Example

we we we we we we we we we we we we we

we we we we we we we we we we we we we

we we we we we we we we we we we we we

we we we we we we we we we we we we we

is is is is is is is is is is is is is is is is is is is is is

is is is is is is is is is is is is is is is is is is is is is

is is is is is is is is is is is is is is is is is is is is is

is is is is is is is is is is is is is is is is is is is is is

us us us us us us us us us us us us us us us us

us us us us us us us us us us us us us us us us

us us us us us us us us us us us us us us us us

us us us us us us us us us us us us us us us us

Repeat the following word 4 lines

1) we

2) is

3) us

4) of

5) if

6) he

7) do

8) war

9) wap

10) eke

11) elf

12) row

13) rue

14) qua

15) quip

16) wale

17) pour

18) rule

19) idol

20) oaks

21) used

22) quire

23) world

24) joker

25) riper

26) odour

27) ideal

28) upper

29) quaker

30) woeful

31) poured

32) rosier

33) opaque

34) jigsaw

35) upward

36) quarrel

37) wakeful

38) prepare

39) ordered

40) jealous

41) failure

42) showers

43) failure

44) showers

45) awkward

46) squalor

47) dawdler

48) foolish

49) khaddar

50) leagued

51) wishful

Exercise 6 (GFTFRF , HJYJUJ)

Typing method

Left Hand fingers

g - Left fore finger   f - Left fore finger

t - Left fore finger   f - Left fore finger

r - Left fore finger   f - Left fore finger

Right Hand fingers

h - Right fore finger   j - Right fore finger

y - Right fore finger   j - Right fore finger

u - Right fore finger   j - Right fore finger

Left Hand Finger Keys on top row

Keep your Left hand finger on keyboard at the position of ... A and
Right hand finger on keyboard ;

Index finger Key........ : **G**

Index finger Key .... : **F**

Index finger Key ...   : **T**

Index finger Key .....   : **F**

Index finger Key .....   : **R**

Index finger Key .....   : **F**

Right Hand Finger Keys on top row

Keep your Right hand finger on keyboard at the position of ... A and Right hand finger on keyboard ;

Index finger Key........ : **H**

Index finger Key........ : **J**

Index finger Key........ : **Y**

Index finger Key........ : **J**

Index finger Key........ : **U**

Index finger Key........ : **J**

Repeat the following 25 lines:

gftfrf   hjyjuj   gftfrf   hjyjuj   gftfrf   hjyjuj   gftfrf   hjyjuj
gftfrf   hjyjuj   gftfrf   hjyjuj   gftfrf   hjyjuj   gftfrf   hjyjuj
gftfrf   hjyjuj   gftfrf   hjyjuj   gftfrf   hjyjuj   gftfrf   hjyjuj
gftfrf   hjyjuj   gftfrf   hjyjuj   gftfrf   hjyjuj   gftfrf   hjyjuj

Exercise 7(GFTFRF HJYJUJ Exercises)

Practicing Method Example

got got got got got got got got got got got got got got
got got got got got got got got got got got got got got
got got got got got got got got got got got got got got
got got got got got got got got got got got got got got

for for for for for for for for for for for for for for
for for for for for for for for for for for for for for
for for for for for for for for for for for for for for
for for for for for for for for for for for for for for

tig tig tig tig tig tig tig tig tig tig tig tig tig tig tig tig
tig tig tig tig tig tig tig tig tig tig tig tig tig tig tig tig
tig tig tig tig tig tig tig tig tig tig tig tig tig tig tig tig
tig tig tig tig tig tig tig tig tig tig tig tig tig tig tig tig

rug rug rug rug rug rug rug rug rug rug rug rug rug rug
rug rug rug rug rug rug rug rug rug rug rug rug rug rug
rug rug rug rug rug rug rug rug rug rug rug rug rug rug
rug rug rug rug rug rug rug rug rug rug rug rug rug rug

Repeat each word 4 lines:

1) got
2) for
3) tig
4) rug
5) hoy
6) yap
7) yet
8) ufo
9) yet
10) ufo
11) ugh
12) joy
13) that
14) they
15) ugly
16) your
17) yogi
18) tree
19) yuft
20) gift
21) high
22) haft
23) legal
24) quote
25) power
26) their
27) there
28) water
29) ghost
30) gypsy
31) hedge
32) kitty
33) writer
34) squire
35) people
36) taught
37) typist
38) lawyer
39) yellow
40) shares
41) uppish
42) letter
43) towards
44) through
45) thought
46) theatre
47) purpose
48) prepare
49) whether
50) shekels
51) geology
52) history
53) authority
54) addressed
55) disfigure
56) supersede
57) therefore

58) yesterday   59) spiritual   60) telegraph

61) etiquette   62) forthwith

Lesson – 3 (Bottom Row)

How to use (Bottom Row)

Z X C V and **M N B** are called to be a bottom row keys.

Keep on your mind:
- Always keep your fingers on **A S D F** and **; L K J.**
- While you are pressing bottom row key, use only corresponding finger. Don't move all the fingers to bottom row.
- Your fingers always kept on **A S D F** and **; L K J** positions.
- While typing bottom Row characters don't see keyboard.
- Your Eyes only focus on moniter
- If you done any mistakes don't try to correct. Just leave your mistakes and continue your fingering on keyboard
- Care about that mistakenly typed characters to reduce your mistakes

Exercise 8 (AZXCVF , LKMNBJ)

Typing method

Left Hand fingers
a - Left little finger

z - Left ring finger

x - Left middle finger

c - Left fore finger

v - Left fore finger

f - Left fore finger

Right Hand fingers
l - Right fore finger

k - Right Middle finger

m - Right Middle finger

n - Right fore finger

b - Right Middle finger   j - Right fore finger

Left Hand Finger Keys Image of bottom row

Right Hand Finger Keys Image

Left Hand Finger Keys on botom row

Keep your Left hand finger on keyboard at the position of ... A and Right hand finger on keyboard ;

Little finger key .... : **A**

Ring finger key ....   : **Z**

Middle finger key ...   : **X**

Index finger key .....   : **C**

Index finger key .....   : **V**

Right Hand Finger Keys on botom row

Keep your Left hand finger on keyboard at the position of ... A and Right hand finger on keyboard ;

Little finger key.........: ;

Ring finger key .... : **L**

Middle finger key ... : **K**

Middle finger key ......: **M**

Index finger key ......: **N**

Index finger key ......: **B**

Repeat the following 25 lines:

azxcvf lkmnbj azxcvf lkmnbj azxcvf lkmnbj azxcvf lkmnbj
azxcvf lkmnbj azxcvf lkmnbj azxcvf lkmnbj azxcvf lkmnbj
azxcvf lkmnbj azxcvf lkmnbj azxcvf lkmnbj azxcvf lkmnbj
azxcvf lkmnbj azxcvf lkmnbj azxcvf lkmnbj azxcvf lkmnbj

Exercise 9 (Bottom Row Exercises)

Practicing Method Example

zonal zonal zonal zonal zonal zonal zonal zonel zonel
zonal zonal zonal zonal zonal zonal zonal zonel zonel
zonal zonal zonal zonal zonal zonal zonal zonel zonel
zonal zonal zonal zonal zonal zonal zonal zonel zonel

zebra zebra zebra zebra zebra zebra zebra zebra zebra
zebra zebra zebra zebra zebra zebra zebra zebra zebra
zebra zebra zebra zebra zebra zebra zebra zebra zebra
zebra zebra zebra zebra zebra zebra zebra zebra zebra

xebec xebec xebec xebec xebec xebec xebec xebec xebc
xebec xebec xebec xebec xebec xebec xebec xebec xebc
xebec xebec xebec xebec xebec xebec xebec xebec xebc
xebec xebec xebec xebec xebec xebec xebec xebec xebc

xylem xylem xylem xylem xylem xylem xylem xylem xylem
xylem xylem xylem xylem xylem xylem xylem xylem xylem
xylem xylem xylem xylem xylem xylem xylem xylem xylem
xylem xylem xylem xylem xylem xylem xylem xylem xylem

Repeat each word 4 lines:

1) zonal	2) zebra	3) xebec
4) xylem	5) cobra	6) crime
7) voice	8) vizov	9) bumpy
10) bunch	11) zenith	12) column
13) naming	14) taxing	15) wizard
16) behalf	17) cheque	18) volume
19) number	20) public	21) cheaply
22) maximum	23) minimum	24) swizzle
25) symbols	26) syringe	27) thunder
28) cobbler	29) machine	30) reneoed
31) foolscap	32) cylinder	33) medicine
34) commonly	35) election	36) mnemonic
37) phonetic	38) monopoly	39) judgment
40) relaxing	41) candidate	42) accompany
43) exemption	44) primitive	45) available
46) amendment	47) movements	48) questions
49) gymnastic	50) nightgown	

Exercise 9 (dot and comma)

Right Hand Finger Keys on botom row

Keep your Left hand finger on keyboard at the position of ... A and Right hand finger on keyboard ;

Little finger key.........: ;

Little finger key .... : .

Ring finger key ... : ,

Typing method

Right Hand fingers

; - Right little finger   . - Right little finger

, - Right ring finger

Right Hand Fingers Position and its Characters

Little Finger : ;	Little Finger : .
	Ring Finger : ,

Dot, comma Exercises

Practicing Method Example

doz., doz., doz., doz., doz., doz., doz., doz., doz., doz.,
doz., doz., doz., doz., doz., doz., doz., doz., doz., doz.,
doz., doz., doz., doz., doz., doz., doz., doz., doz., doz.,
doz., doz., doz., doz., doz., doz., doz., doz., doz., doz.,

etc., etc., etc., etc., etc., etc., etc., etc., etc., etc., etc.,
etc., etc., etc., etc., etc., etc., etc., etc., etc., etc., etc.,
etc., etc., etc., etc., etc., etc., etc., etc., etc., etc., etc.,
etc., etc., etc., etc., etc., etc., etc., etc., etc., etc., etc.,

viz., viz., viz., viz., viz., viz., viz., viz., viz., viz., viz., viz., viz.,
viz., viz., viz., viz., viz., viz., viz., viz., viz., viz., viz., viz., viz.,
viz., viz., viz., viz., viz., viz., viz., viz., viz., viz., viz., viz., viz.,
viz., viz., viz., viz., viz., viz., viz., viz., viz., viz., viz., viz., viz.,

Repeat each word 4 lines

1) doz.,   2) etc.,   3) viz.,

4) govt.,   5) misc.,   6) bldg.,

7) necy.,   8) estt.,   9) dept.,

10) secv.,

Left & Right Hand Finger Keys Overall View

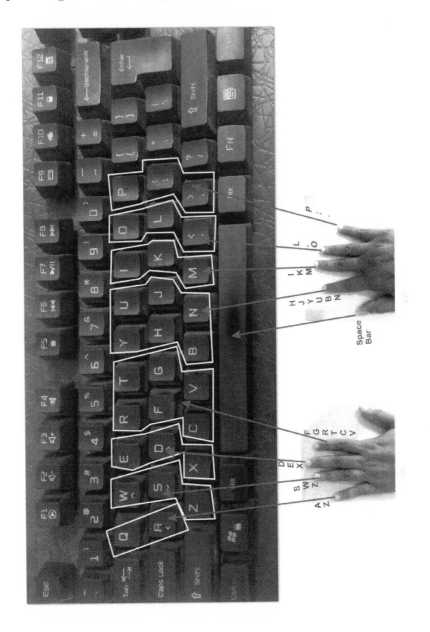

Exercise 10 (A to Z and Z to A Practice)

Repeat the following 25 lines ; But hereafter daily type 10 lines before commencing to type anything

abcdedfghijklmnopqrstuvwxyz.,   zyxwvutsrqponmlkjihgfedcba,.

abcdedfghijklmnopqrstuvwxyz.,   zyxwvutsrqponmlkjihgfedcba,.

abcdedfghijklmnopqrstuvwxyz.,   zyxwvutsrqponmlkjihgfedcba,.

abcdedfghijklmnopqrstuvwxyz.,   zyxwvutsrqponmlkjihgfedcba,.

abcdedfghijklmnopqrstuvwxyz.,   zyxwvutsrqponmlkjihgfedcba,.

abcdedfghijklmnopqrstuvwxyz.,   zyxwvutsrqponmlkjihgfedcba,.

abcdedfghijklmnopqrstuvwxyz.,   zyxwvutsrqponmlkjihgfedcba,.

abcdedfghijklmnopqrstuvwxyz.,   zyxwvutsrqponmlkjihgfedcba,.

abcdedfghijklmnopqrstuvwxyz.,   zyxwvutsrqponmlkjihgfedcba,.

abcdedfghijklmnopqrstuvwxyz.,   zyxwvutsrqponmlkjihgfedcba,.

Exercise 11

Practicing Method Example

balance   balance   balance   balance   balance   balance   balance
balance   balance   balance   balance   balance   balance   balance
balance   balance   balance   balance   balance   balance   balance
balance   balance   balance   balance   balance   balance   balance

careful careful careful careful careful careful careful careful
careful careful careful careful careful careful careful careful
careful careful careful careful careful careful careful careful
careful careful careful careful careful careful careful careful

subject subject subject subject subject subject subject
subject subject subject subject subject subject subject
subject subject subject subject subject subject subject
subject subject subject subject subject subject subject

stomach stomach stomach stomach stomach stomach
stomach stomach stomach stomach stomach stomach
stomach stomach stomach stomach stomach stomach
stomach stomach stomach stomach stomach stomach

Repeat each word 4 lines

1) balance   2) careful   3) subject

4) stomach   5) thunder   6) process

7) between   8) nominee   9) voyaged

10)middav   11) xylophone   12) yieldable

13) secretary   14) effective   15) clockwise

16) primitive   17) signature   18) coworker

19) milk maid   20) tomorrow   21) commission

22) department   23) government   24) hereditary

25)atmosphere   26)qualifying   27)zoological

28)possession   29)complement   30)monotomous

31) questioning   32) corporation   33)performance

34) thoughtless   35) view finder   36) democracies

37) incorporate   38) incorporate   39) familiarity

40) anniversary   41) hureaucracy

Lesson – 4 (Number Row)

How to use (Number Row)

1 2 3 4 5 and **0 9 8 7 6 7** are called to be a number row keys.

Keep on your mind:
- Always keep your fingers on **A S D F** and **; L K J.**
- While you are pressing number row key, use only corresponding finger. Don't move all the fingers to number row.
- Your fingers always kept on **A S D F** and **; L K J** positions.
- While typing number row numbers don't see keyboard.
- Your Eyes only focus on moniter
- If you done any mistakes don't try to correct. Just leave your mistakes and continue your fingering on keyboard
- Care about that mistakenly typed numbers to reduce your mistakes

Exercise 12 (123454 098767)

Typing method

Left Hand fingers

1 - Left little finger	2 - Left ring finger
3 - Left middle finger	4 - Left fore finger
5 - Left fore finger	

Right Hand fingers

0 - Right little finger	9 - Right ring finger
8 - Right Middle finger	7 - Right fore finger

6 - Right fore finger

Left Hand Finger Keys Image of Number row

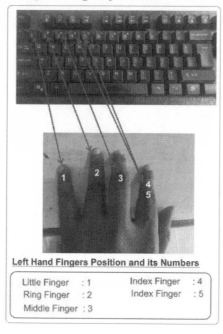

Left Hand Fingers Position and its Numbers

Little Finger : 1	Index Finger : 4	
Ring Finger : 2	Index Finger : 5	
Middle Finger : 3		

Right Hand Finger Keys Image of Number row

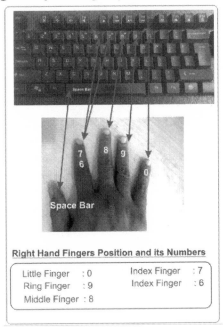

Right Hand Fingers Position and its Numbers

Little Finger	: 0	Index Finger	: 7
Ring Finger	: 9	Index Finger	: 6
Middle Finger	: 8		

Repeat the following 25 lines:

123454 098767 123454 098767 123454 098767
123454 098767 123454 098767 123454 098767
123454 098767 123454 098767 123454 098767
123454 098767 123454 098767 123454 098767

Exercise 13 (Number Exercise)

Practicing Method Example

1945 1945 1945 1945 1945 1945 1945 1945 1945
1945 1945 1945 1945 1945 1945 1945 1945 1945
1945 1945 1945 1945 1945 1945 1945 1945 1945
1945 1945 1945 1945 1945 1945 1945 1945 1945

1956 1956 1956 1956 1956 1956 1956 1956 1956 1956
1956 1956 1956 1956 1956 1956 1956 1956 1956 1956
1956 1956 1956 1956 1956 1956 1956 1956 1956 1956
1956 1956 1956 1956 1956 1956 1956 1956 1956 1956

1975 1975 1975 1975 1975 1975 1975 1975 1975
1975 1975 1975 1975 1975 1975 1975 1975 1975
1975 1975 1975 1975 1975 1975 1975 1975 1975
1975 1975 1975 1975 1975 1975 1975 1975 1975

1980 1980 1980 1980 1980 1980 1980 1980 1980
1980 1980 1980 1980 1980 1980 1980 1980 1980
1980 1980 1980 1980 1980 1980 1980 1980 1980
1980 1980 1980 1980 1980 1980 1980 1980 1980

Repeat each word 4 lines

1) 1945   2)1956   3) 1975

4) 1980   5) 1985   6) 1986

7) 1987   8) 1988   9) 1989

10) 1990   11) 2012   12) 2017

13) 2019   14) 2020   15) 2025

Exercise 14 (Number with dot and comma Exercise)

VARIOUS WAYS OF PUNCTUATING FIGURES

Practicing Method Example

1,78,64,532.53 1,78,64,532.53 1,78,64,532.53 1,78,64,532.53

1,78,64,532.53 1,78,64,532.53 1,78,64,532.53 1,78,64,532.53

1,78,64,532.53 1,78,64,532.53 1,78,64,532.53 1,78,64,532.53

1,78,64,532.53 1,78,64,532.53 1,78,64,532.53 1,78,64,532.53

2,62,84651.92 2,62,84651.92 2,62,84651.92 2,62,84651.92

2,62,84651.92 2,62,84651.92 2,62,84651.92 2,62,84651.92

2,62,84651.92 2,62,84651.92 2,62,84651.92 2,62,84651.92

2,62,84651.92 2,62,84651.92 2,62,84651.92 2,62,84651.92

17,864,532.53 17,864,532.53 17,864,532.53 17,864,532.53

17,864,532.53 17,864,532.53 17,864,532.53 17,864,532.53

17,864,532.53 17,864,532.53 17,864,532.53 17,864,532.53

17,864,532.53 17,864,532.53 17,864,532.53 17,864,532.53

Repeat each word 4 lines

1) 1,78,64,532.53   2) 2,62,84651.92

3) 17,864,532.53   4) 26,284,651.92

5) 178,64,53,2.53   6) 2,628,46,51.92

7) 1,78,645,32.53   8) 2,62,846,51.92

9) 1,78,64,532.53   10) 2,62,84,651.92

Lesson – 5 (Capital Letters)

How to use of Capital Letters

- Left side Shift Key is to be pressed to type a capital letter on the right side of the Key Board
- Right side Shift Key is to be pressed to type a capital letter on the left side of the Key Board

Typing method

Left Shift Key
Left side Shift Key + Right side characters

Right Shift Key
Right side Shift Key + Left side characters

Exercise 15 (Captial Letters Exercise)

Practicing Method Example

Sunday   Sunday   Sunday   Sunday   Sunday   Sunday   Sunday
Sunday   Sunday   Sunday   Sunday   Sunday   Sunday   Sunday
Sunday   Sunday   Sunday   Sunday   Sunday   Sunday   Sunday
Sunday   Sunday   Sunday   Sunday   Sunday   Sunday   Sunday

Monday   Monday   Monday   Monday   Monday   Monday
Monday   Monday   Monday   Monday   Monday   Monday
Monday   Monday   Monday   Monday   Monday   Monday
Monday   Monday   Monday   Monday   Monday   Monday

Repeat each word 4 lines

1) Sunday

2) Monday

3) Tuesday

4) Wednesday

5) Thursday

6) Friday

7) Saturday

8) 1ST January 1980

9) 14th October 1985

10) January

11) February

12) March

13) April

14) May

15) June

16) July

17) August

18) September

19) October

20) December

21) New Delhi

22) Tamil Nadu

23) America

24) Japan

25) Calcutta

26) Malasiya

27) Singapore

28) Iran

29) Iraq

30) Government

31) Department

32) Superintendent

33) Deputy

34) Additional

35) Inspector – General

36) Accountant – General

37) 3rd March 1984

38) 10th April 1991

Lesson – 6 (Other Keys)

No need to practice. But use it...

Caps Lock   : Left Little finger

Tab   : Left Little finger

~   : Left Little finger

Esc   : Left Little finger

Ctrl   : Left Little finger

/   : Right Little finger

\   : Right Little finger

[: Right Little finger

]   : Right Little finger

-              : Right Little finger

Backspace   : Right Little finger

?   : Left little finger (shift key) + Right little finger?

>   : Left little finger (shift key) + Right little finger?

<   : Left little finger (shift key) + Right ring finger?

Exercise 16 (Exercise for All the keys)

Practicing Method Example

Pack my box with five dozen liquor jugs.
Pack my box with five dozen liquor jugs.
Pack my box with five dozen liquor jugs.
Pack my box with five dozen liquor jugs.

Pack my box with five dozen liquor jugs.
Pack my box with five dozen liquor jugs.
Pack my box with five dozen liquor jugs.
Pack my box with five dozen liquor jugs.

The quick brown fox slyly jumped over the lazy dog.
The quick brown fox slyly jumped over the lazy dog.
The quick brown fox slyly jumped over the lazy dog.
The quick brown fox slyly jumped over the lazy dog.

The quick brown fox slyly jumped over the lazy dog.
The quick brown fox slyly jumped over the lazy dog.
The quick brown fox slyly jumped over the lazy dog.
The quick brown fox slyly jumped over the lazy dog.

Petty quiz badly vexes chuffy worker, hungry James.
Petty quiz badly vexes chuffy worker, hungry James.
Petty quiz badly vexes chuffy worker, hungry James.
Petty quiz badly vexes chuffy worker, hungry James.

Petty quiz badly vexes chuffy worker, hungry James.
Petty quiz badly vexes chuffy worker, hungry James.
Petty quiz badly vexes chuffy worker, hungry James.

Petty quiz badly vexes chuffy worker, hungry James.

Repeat 20 times each of the following sentences
1. Pack my box with five dozen liquor jugs.
2. The quick brown fox slyly jumped over the lazy dog.
3. Petty quiz badly vexes chuffy worker, hungry James.
4. May we have Jack squires fix the big lamps for Andy Ziegler?
5. Did James get very few boxes of this size opened so quickly?
6. Will Van and Joe pick the six-men for my big quiz?
7. Handy Jack's quixotic laziness may grow to be far expensive
8. Hal Ritz was requested to pick five or six new Judges by May.
9. John Quickly extemporizes five wooden bags
10. Gay men with extra pluck and zeal would often have quiet jobs.
11. When dusk fell they know they must just wait till help came
12. Put your best heart into your work and pull with all your might
13. Each time they come near this city they feel they must stay
14. The Best Day is today . The greatest Sin is Fear.
15. The Best Gift is Fovgiveness. The Meanest feeling is Jealousy.
16. The Greatest Need is commonsense. The most expensive indulgence is Hate
17. The Cleverest man is one who does what he thinks right.
18. The worst bankrupt is the soul that has lost its enthusiasm
19. The Cheapest, Stupidest, Easiest thing to do is Finding Fault
20. Get up early and pray to God for the welfare of all.

Lesson – 6 (Spacing Rules)

What is the Spacing Rules

- Leave **ONE SPACE** after **:**
  Comma **(,)** , Semi – Colon (;), Colon (:)
- Leave **TWO SPACE** after :
  Full – sop (.) , Question Mark (?), Exclamation Mark (!)
- Leave **NO SPACE** before or after a:
  Dash (--)

Leave FIVE SPACES for commenceing a: Paragraph

Exercise 17 (Use Spacing Rules)

Practicing Method Example

The present Gulf War has affected more than 5,00,000 Indians.
The present Gulf War has affected more than 5,00,000 Indians.
The present Gulf War has affected more than 5,00,000 Indians.
The present Gulf War has affected more than 5,00,000 Indians.

The present Gulf War has affected more than 5,00,000 Indians.
The present Gulf War has affected more than 5,00,000 Indians.
The present Gulf War has affected more than 5,00,000 Indians.
The present Gulf War has affected more than 5,00,000 Indians.

75% of India's population live in villages.
75% of India's population live in villages.
75% of India's population live in villages.
75% of India's population live in villages.

Repeat 10 times each of the following sentences

1. The present Gulf War has affected more than 5,00,000 Indians.
2. 75% of India's population live in villages.
3. A cheeque for Rs.500/- ws drawn on M/s. Rman & Co., Madras.
4. The Income Tax Department allows 15% depreciation on Machinery
5. The Typist said, "I want to type this letter within ½ an hour."
6. The plaintain is cultivated on ¼th of the land and 3/4th is for paddy.
7. The exchange rate $1 is about Rs.64 Only
8. Sindhuja paid $150 as custom's duty.
9. Lalitha (alias) Veena Captained the Badminton team.
10. Raja was admitted in the hospital; he was taken to intensive care unit.
11. "Procrastination is the thief of time" – remember this too.
12. Have patience: "Rome wasnot built in a day"
13. Ram & Rahim Shared the profits and losses in the ratio of 3:2.
14. Oh! What a beautiful flower it is!

Exercise 18 (Paragraph Practice 1)

Type the following paragraph 5 times

What causes left-handedness? there are many theories. Some say it is inherited; others, that it is a result of habit, education and environment. Most scientists, however, believe that left-handedness has a biological basis. It is known that the left hemisphere of the brain controls the right half of the body and the right hemisphere, the left. Most of us are right handed because in most of us it is the left hemisphere that is dominant. In those who are left-handed, it is the right hemisphere of the brain that is dominant. If there is no dominance ofeither hemisphere over the other then the person might become ambidextrous. An American Psychiatrist, Dr.Camilla Benbow has found that many students who are exceptionally good at Mathametics are left-handed. She says this is due to the dominanace of the right hemisphere which is the seat of mathematical reasoning abilty

Exercise 19 (Paragraph Practice 2)

Type the following paragraph 5 times each (Leave FIVE SPACES before commencing a paragraph)

A ballon rises because it is lighter than the body of air which it displaces. It is forced upwards by the difference between the upward and downward pressure of the air on it. Man first went up in a balloon form Paris. The balloon attained a height of 90 metres approximately, and came to earth about 3.2 Kilometres from the starting point.

All of you must have listened to the sounds produced by a guitar, veena or tabla! Musical Instruments produce sound waves. These travel throught the air and cause vibrations in our eardrums. On table, mridangam, etc., which are percussion instruments, vibration is produced by the hand when it strikes the instrument. As far as the flute, shehnai, etc., are concerned, you must have seen players blowing inot them. That is what produces the sound waves causing the eardrums to vibrate.

Exercise 20 (Paragraph Practice 3)

Type the following paragraph 10 times

Every one must accept the fact that discipline among students, workers and persons in public life is of an absolute necessity for progress. When certain rules are framed it must be understood that it is not to harass any individual; similarly there should not be any suspicion in our minds that it is against any particular person.

Generally, in the common interest certain rules are framed and as students if they are trained to follow the same they are only helped in their life. Initially it may appear little bit difficult for anybody to follow the rules, but every individual will realize that the disciplined life will be primarily responsible for his progress in future. Every honest citizen of the country feel that we must subject ourselves to certain restricitions so that the society can be purified and ultimately a better discipline can be maintained at the national level.

The Institutes which are coaching the students for job oriented courses has got a greater responsibility to educate the students of their moral obligations to the society. It is in this context, we, as an Institute, attach more importance for the maintenance of discipline, in the interest of the Institute and students. Students can be assured of bright future if they get themselves trained in an atmosphere of this nature, and one can have unshakable confidence that this alone can help him for the future thought initially it may appear to be little bit difficult.

Exercise 21 (Paragraph Practice 4)

Type the following paragraph 10 times

Students can help the Institutes to function effectively to cater the needs of candidates by remitting the fees in time without making it a burden for the instructors of the Institutes to repeatedly work on it. It may be surprising for the students as to how this can facilitate for the smooth functioning of the Institute. By your experience you must have seen within a short span of time of one period either, 45 minutes or one hour, the instructors have to mark the attendance, attend the students, correct the papers and answer the queries of the parents. With this load of work all unproductive work must definitely be eliminated. When the fees, that is however going to be paid, is paid within first five working days, the students get the benefit of the instructors fully concentrating on them. Further when bulk of the students remitting sufficiently in advance, little number of students who delay it are responsible for the students losing the benefit of availing the service of the instructors. During the examination period the instructors can do a better job instead of simply taking the list of arrears of fees, reminding them frequently and take steps to collect the dues.

Exercise 22 (Paragraph Practice 5)

Type the following paragraph 10 times

Students are the best lot of beneficiary by handling the typewriters carefully. It is not difficult to attend to the defects of the machine in the class. But if the defects can be reduced by avoiding defective operation to a large extent, students will have the full advantage of practicing in the same typewriter without any interruption. The qualitative performance of the typewriter is an encouraging factor to the students. He will be more pleased in working on a typewriter which functions smoothly to his satisfaction. Students should basically realize that in handling the typewriter carefully he is helping himself more than helping the institutes. If they realize this concept and cultivate the habit of taking all precautions it helps them during the examination. The last batch candidates fate should not be decided by the first batch candidates in handling the machine. When machines are handled carefully students can certainly avaod the risk of any defects being rectified during the examination. Therefore it is now clear that while it may be easy for an institute to attend to the defects with their mechanic it is only difficult for the students during their practice and examination which can certainly be avoided by realizing the imperative need of handling the typewriter carefully

Exercise 23 (Paragraph Practice 6)

Type the following paragraph 10 times

Commerce education is a very short course, training the candidates with an academic qualification of ten years so as to enable them to fit in an organization, either government or private. What is important is not only to learn that are required for administrative procedures but on top of it to cultivate certain good habits to help themselves to be successful in the official career. Among other things one of the important requirements is to maintain punctuality. Punctuality is a thing that can easily be followed. But basically we must practice to be punctual. If at all people are not punctual it is mainly because they must have cultivated the habit of late-coming ignoring the need to report on time. Anybody who is punctual will always be practicing it in their life at any cost. Late-reporting and delaying is a very irksome one and it will be a point of irritation while dealing with the public. In that process people become non-acceptable and that leads to failures however talented one may be. With this background we enfornce punctuality among the students so that while learning they actually practice and learn to be punctual. When you come to the class punctually you are not tired and naturally your performance in First Paper would be better. If you are coming in a hurry and type in an exhausted manner you will commit more mistakes. when you get yourself accustomed to behave in this manner and as a person not caring to be punctual, it cannot be rectified later. A student who is accustomed to commit more mistakes cannot become an efficient typist. When you lose time of your usual practice you will not be doing real justice and the degree of performance will go down. It is not a question of your attending the class all days but whether you have done your job all the time in toto is required

Exercise 24 (Paragraph Practice 7)

Type the following paragraph 10 times

India is a country with all resournces and can certainly compete with anybody in the world. Unfortunately people do not seem to realize the need to respect the values. This tendency at home leads to ignore the national interest. In olden days elders are considered to be essential, whereas today it is otherwise considered as a burden. It is mainly because the younger generation do not tolerate interference. Interference is only in their own interest but the students do not consider the interference as a good thing to them. Nothing can be alright when it is not checked. Once we accept in life that checking is nothing short of a chalking out a good plan that will not lead to a wrong conclusion. Our past literature has proved how elders were respected, parents were respected and teachers were respected. All those who were respecting were able to be successful in their life. How it happended? When once we accept and respect the elders it is not only a personal respect. In other words we love their ideas, we believe their policies, we attach importance in their handling things. Therefore we are more inclinded to take them as our leadaers and we are immensely pleased to follow them in life. Once this is done we get a good lead and the fact we follow them we are also getting ourselves improved. The confidence once can have in the leadership is basically as a result of the belief and respect he has developed within himself. By cultivating this good habit of respecting their teachers, respecting the institution and elders the students will have the benefit of practicing good things and habitually they will be wedded to good habits. That will make them more successful in their life.

Exercise 25 (Paragraph Practice 8)

Type the following paragraph 10 times

People are under the wrong impression that many unemployed youth with commerce education are still not absorbed and ask whether there is any real need to further equip themselves with commerce education. It is a wrong notion since no Government or organization can assure 100% employment opportunity. Can we afford to stop going to schools because many matriculates are still unemployed. Everybody is clear in their mind that they must be basically qualified first to appear before any interview when occasion arises. Similarly commerce education plays a major role. In fact, out of the total unemployed segment mere academic qualification has not solved their problems. It is only those who have Typewriting – Shorthand qualification stands a better chance. It is proved that the commerce education, thought the course may be short-ranging from six months to one year, only shape the person with an academic qualification of twelve years to fit in an organization. It is now clear that the commerce education plays a major role in securing employment. Similarly, commerce education facilitate to be self-reliant if somebody does not want to serve under anybody. They can certainly be self-employed. When we talk of self-employement more than anything else it is the commerce education that helps them to a great extent. If you look at the prestigious points of occupation you can certainly be convinced that it is only those who learn Shorthand and Typewriting can be Personal Assistants to Ministers, Personal Secretaries to big industrialists, P.As. to Judges and Personal Clerks to Officers, who can shape the economy of the country. The management, both in private and public sector, has to rely for all confidential work only on their stenographers. The people who acquire the knowledge of Twin Arts are able to serve, the community better and they can certainly claim that they have made their useful contribution to the society in improving the productivity and the economic conditions of the country

About the Author

G.Shiva is the properator cum faculty of cgsinfotech . Cgs infotech is a computer education centre.

Now days most of the people use computers. But they take more time to type the single page of content. They struggle to type the characters. They interested to learn keyboard typing. but they do not able spend time in education centre. So author plan to write a book for those people who interested to learn keyboard typing in their home or office

If you buy this book when ever you think to learn keyboard typing, you can use it. you can learn it your house or office. Just spent 10 to 20 minutes every day. with in a month you will become expert of your keys.

Author has 20 years experience in software education, web designing, teaching grammar and spoken english courses.

The author also a famous youtuber in tamilnadu. Many students follow his channel for study purpose. He has own matrimony website for matrimony services.

He developed more than 10 websites to his customers now he enter in kindle publishing to share his knowledge worldwide this is authors second book. So if you have doubts or if you found any mistakes please mail us at gsrasi2006@yahoo.co.in

Authors other book

1) Speak English

Talk English : 1000 Common English sentences for native speakers

Url Link : https://goo.gl/8V2LqQ

One Last Thing ....

If you enjoyed this book or found it useful i'd be very greateful. If you'd post a short review on Amazon. Your support really does make a difference and i read all the reviews personally so i can get your feedback and make this book even better

Thanks again for your support

Made in the USA
Monee, IL
15 September 2020